MW01491540

Single to Married

30 Days of Transformation, Restoration, and Healing

DEVOTIONAL

Chloe M. Gooden

Single to Married

Copyright 2013 Chloe M. Gooden

All rights reserved.

All rights reserved. No part of this book may be reproduced in any form, except for the inclusion of brief quotations in a review, without permission in writing from the author or publisher.

ISBN-13:978-1499633351

ISBN-10:1499633351

Also available in eBook

Cover Design: Diango Lando

Author Photo : Daria L. Blevins

Need answers or advice? Message Me on Facebook @

https://www.facebook.com/ChloeMGooden

PRINTED IN THE UNITED STATES OF AMERICA

Copyright © 2014 Chloe M. Gooden

All rights reserved.

Acknowledgments

To my family who has always been there for me through every trial, blessing, and struggle in my life. I don't know where I would be if God hadn't blessed me with your love and support. Thank you for always being here for me. I love you more than anything.

Love,
Chloe M. Gooden

Introduction

Psalm 139: 23-24

"Search me, O God, and know my heart; Try me and know my anxious thoughts; And see if there be any hurtful way in me, And lead me in the everlasting way."

Any time we attempt to change something about ourselves— physically, mentally, or spiritually—we try to find the quickest way to make that change so we can go to the next project. We look for any book, blog, or internet source and find the quickest way to make the change happen instantly. Our eyes are fixated on the headlines "Lose 10 pounds in 10 Days!" or "In 30 Days, Lose All Your Wrinkles." Whatever it may be, we want the quick fix! Well I am here to tell you that any type of transformation that you want in your life takes time and patience. Nothing can be done as a quick fix. A quick fix is always a temporary fix. If you want any type of transformation in your life it takes discipline and a true commitment to change. In this *30 Days of Transformation, Restoration, and Healing*, there are daily prayers and reflections to help you start transitioning mentally, emotionally, and spiritually from a single woman to a potential wife; but most of all, a woman that is healed and restored.

Notice I said it will *help you start*. Truly encompassing this woman takes not just 30 days, but a continuous effort to be all God has designed you to be. Take each day and truly take hold of the scripture and questions, sit back, and think about the areas of improvement you need to make. Pray on each topic and ask God to search your heart. We all are in need of healing and restoration in some area of our lives and in the process, you will transform into a better woman. What better time to do it than now?

Each day I have given you a prayer starter for the day. You can tweak this any way that you like and I leave room for you to add the personal issues you may be dealing with on each topic. Prayer is a big part of your transformation and intimacy with God. Take time to talk with God daily and He will begin revealing areas in your life that need His divine anointing. Understand that God loves you tremendously and you can talk to Him just like you would a best friend or counselor. I started the prayers for you, but ensure to make the prayers your own. The way your relationship is with God, is dependent on you and the time you spend with Him.

Truly meditate on each topic and the questions. Ask God to search your heart and reveal to you what He sees. If you skip a day, no worries! Just start where you left off! Some of the issues you may come across in the topics may take you more than just a day of reflecting. That is completely fine. If you want to, you can take each topic weekly so you can take time out to let the change resonate in your heart, mind, body and soul. I pray that these devotional topics free you from any hurt and pain you have been dealing with and also help you change your life

Philippians 4:13 *"I can do all things through Christ who strengthens me..."*

Table of Contents

Day 1

Trust God

<u>Psalm 37:3–6</u> *"Trust in the Lord, and do good; dwell in the land and befriend faithfulness. Delight yourself in the Lord, and he will give you the desires of your heart. Commit your way to the Lord; trust in him, and he will act. He will bring forth your righteousness as the light, and your justice as the noonday..."*

~Prayer Starter~

'Lord, throughout this entire process of healing, restoration, and transformation I pray that you help me to be patient and trust that everything I pray about is done in Jesus Name. Build my faith up in you and help me realize that everything you did for those in the Bible, you will do for me as well. You will heal me. You will restore my family. You will help me be a better steward of my finances. You will help me forget my past hurts, transgressions, and regrets. You will mold me into the woman you've called me to be. Everything I pray for in Jesus Name is already done. Remind me of how faithful you have already been in my life and always keep in mind that you are the same God yesterday, today, and forevermore..."

~ Reflection ~

What do you want the most from your daily prayers and devotion? Do you believe that God hears you and can do all that you have asked for? Where are you struggling with your faith? As you go through the devotionals the key to a change in your life is having FAITH that God can do all that you have asked for. Without faith you can't be pleasing to God because you don't trust Him. Trust God. He will always do as He says. He will NEVER fail you.

Hebrews 11:6 *"And without faith it is impossible to please God, because anyone who comes to him must believe that he exists and that he rewards those who earnestly seek him..."*

_____

_____

_____

_____

_____

_____

_____

_____

_____

_____

_____

_____

Day 2

Search Me

Psalm 139:23 *"Search me, God, and know my heart; test me and know my anxious thoughts..."*

~ Prayer Starter ~

"God, search my heart and show me the areas that I need to work on and the areas you know I need to change. I've been by myself for a while and it's hard to notice the things that I need to adjust for a spouse to enter my life. Beyond meeting a spouse, I want to please you and be the woman you've called me to be whether I am single or getting married. Lord, help me to remain strong in the transition and to trust you in the process. Help me to be patient and trust your timing."

~ Reflection ~

What areas of improvement are you aware of currently that you can work on? What can you do to work on this area now? Think of times where you've received constructive criticism. What did they reveal to you?

Reaching within ourselves and finding the areas that need pruning can be a hard process. We all have areas where we can be better spiritually, mentally, physically, and emotionally. Though it is hard sometimes to become vulnerable to the criticism and conviction, it is necessary to truly see change. The best part about it is that, regardless of what the iniquity may be, God is forgiving and willing to give us the strength to change and become more like Christ.

Day 3

Patience

Psalm 40:1 *"I waited patiently and expectantly for the Lord; and He inclined to me and heard my cry..."*

~Prayer Starter~

"God, show me the areas where I am impatient with your timing and ultimately not trusting you. Help me to understand the importance of being patient and the importance of building endurance in my wait. Show me why I am so anxious and why I am having trouble trusting your timing and wisdom. Help me to wait and realize that there is a season for everything and you know when it is the right time to fulfill my desires and calling."

~ Reflection ~

What areas in your life are you becoming anxious about? Why are you impatient about it and why do you feel you need it now? Why are you having a hard time trusting God's timing for what you have asked for?

Patience is one of the fruits of the spirit and needed most when fulfilling God's calling over your life. Many prophesies, callings, or any other task ordained by God takes time and patience to develop and nurture. He is never late and rarely early. Trust His timing. Ask Him to help you be content and wait for Him.

Day 4

Contentment

__Philippians 4:12__ *"I know what it is to be in need, and I know what it is to have plenty. I have learned the secret of being content in any and every situation, whether well fed or hungry, whether living in plenty or in want..."*

~Prayer Starter~

"God, thank you for all that you've given me and the many blessings you are continuing to bestow upon my life. I am constantly thinking of the next thing I want or the next thing I want to do and finding myself becoming ungrateful for what you have already given me. Lord help me to have contentment regardless of what I have or where you have me presently. Help me to be like Paul and find the joy in every situation I am presented with in my life. You have a purpose in every season of my life, though sometimes I may not understand it. Help me to be aware of the lesson in each moment and change as a person instead of trying to change the situation..."

~ Reflection ~

Write down everything God has blessed you with presently. What are some things you desire from God? If He never changed your situation, or give you more than you have presently, would you still love and glorify Him?

Learning to appreciate what we have around us is difficult for many of us. Sometimes in our efforts to become more, we forget to appreciate what is around us momentarily and become ungrateful. Though it is great to have goals to aspire to, we need not ever forget what He has given us now.

_____

_____

_____

_____

_____

_____

_____

_____

_____

_____

_____

_____

Day 5

Submit

<u>**1 Peter 3: 1-2, 7**</u> *"Wives, in the same way submit yourselves to your own husbands so that, if any of them do not believe the word, they may be won over without words by the behavior of their wives, [2] when they see the purity and reverence of your lives.... Husbands, in the same way be considerate as you live with your wives, and treat them with respect as the weaker partner and as heirs with you of the gracious gift of life, so that nothing will hinder your prayers...."*

~Prayer Starter~

"Being single I have had to depend on myself for a lot of things and find it hard to grasp the idea of being submissive to a man. I have never been able to trust a man to take care of things and don't quite feel comfortable trusting a man in this way. Your Word says that I should submit to my potential husband and I want to do as you command and trust the order you have placed. God, help me to trust my potential husband. Remind me that he loves me and will only do what's best for me and our family. Help me to understand what it truly means to submit and find a balance in my future marriage. Mold me now into this woman and prepare me for this role..."

~ Reflection ~

Why is it hard for you to trust a man with your life in marriage? What areas would be the hardest for you to give up control? What fears do you have about being submissive? Compare what the world says about being submissive to what God says.

_____

_____

_____

_____

_____

_____

_____

_____

_____

_____

_____

_____

Day 6

Healing

Jeremiah 17:14 *"Heal me, O Lord, and I shall be healed; save me, and I shall be saved, for you are my praise..."*

~Prayer Starter~

"Lord, I have some past hurts that have been hard for me to deal with and still need your healing to take place. I want to be able to heal from these wrongdoings so I can move on and be whole in you and in marriage. You Word says over and over again that you will heal your children and that we can cast our cares on you because you care for me. Lord, heal me from (Insert person that hurt you) and what he did to me. Help me to let go (Insert the action that was done) and move on with my life into the life of freedom and joy and forgiveness. Set me free now in Jesus name and help me to not bring it to remembrance any longer..."

~ Reflection ~

What transgressions of the past are you still holding on to? Do you want to become healed of these past hurts? Find other scriptures on healing and speak them over yourself. Every time you find yourself focusing on the affliction speak your healing scripture and be reminded that God has restored you.

Day 7

Unconditional Love

<u>1 Corinthians 13:4–8</u> *"Love is patient, love is kind, it is not envious. Love does not brag, it is not puffed up.* [5] *It is not rude, it is not self-serving, it is not easily angered or resentful.* [6] *It is not glad about injustice, but rejoices in the truth.* [7] *It bears all things, believes all things, hopes all things, endures all things. Love never ends..."*

~Prayer Starter~

"Lord, thank you for loving me the way you do. Thank you for loving me so much that you sent your Son to die on the cross just for me. You are the perfect example of unconditional love towards us. God, I have loved before and have been loved but, God, help me to understand the difference between love and unconditional love. Help me to understand what it means to love someone so much that I sacrifice my own wants and needs for the other. When I make a commitment to be with my future husband I want to be able to stay in my marriage regardless of how I may feel, or if some things have changed. God, you always have open arms towards me and show me grace. Help me to show the same grace towards others..."

~ Reflection ~

Think about your past relationships, whether intimate or platonic, that you felt you were lacking one of the characteristics of love explained in

Corinthians 13. How can you work on developing these characteristics? What holds you back from giving unconditional love? Have you ever experienced unconditional love?

_____

_____

_____

_____

_____

_____

_____

_____

_____

_____

_____

_____

_____

Day 8

Confidence

Psalm 139:13–14 *"For you created my inmost being; you knit me together in my mother's womb. I praise you because I am fearfully and wonderfully made, your works are wonderful, I know that full well..."*

1 Peter 3:3–4 *"Your beauty should not come from outward adornment, such as braided hair and the wearing of gold jewelry and fine clothes. Instead, it should be that of your inner self, the unfading beauty of a gentle and quiet spirit, which is of great worth in God's sight..."*

~Prayer Starter~

"Lord, it says in your Word that you created me in my mother's womb and that I am fearfully and wonderfully made. God, help me to see myself the way you see me. Help me to not focus on my flaws and focus on the great things you have placed in me that no other human being can possess. Help me to realize that it is not about comparing myself physically to others but to focus on being a woman that pleases your sight. In the areas that I am insecure, help me to be secure in your sight and not compare myself to what the world defines as attractive but to become more concerned about what you see as an honorable woman..."

~ Reflection ~

What insecurities do you have about yourself physically? Why do you find yourself insecure about them? Compare what the world says about you to what the Word says about you. Write down the Bible definition of a virtuous, beautiful woman and keep this in mind when you find yourself comparing your beauty to others.

_____

_____

_____

_____

_____

_____

_____

_____

_____

_____

_____

_____

Day 9

Stewardship

Luke 16: 10-12 *"Whoever can be trusted with very little can also be trusted with much, and whoever is dishonest with very little will also be dishonest with much. [11] So if you have not been trustworthy in handling worldly wealth, who will trust you with true riches? [12] And if you have not been trustworthy with someone else's property, who will give you property of your own?...*

~Prayer Starter~

"God, for the past couple of years I have had to only provide for myself and only consider myself in finances. I felt that I budget my money well but didn't understand the importance of giving back to you and also ensuring that I handled what you'd given me in a way that is pleasing to your sight. God, show me the best way to handle my finances, how to be a faithful tither, and also learn to be a cheerful giver. Show me areas that I can give more now and be a good steward of my resources for your glory. Help me to mature in this area and be a helpmate to my potential spouse in handling our finances as a home..."

~ Reflection ~

What debts do you have currently? What can you do to be rid of your debt and be a lender and not a borrower? Do you budget your money well? Look into some resources such as Dave Ramsay or Crown Financial to learn the best practices in handling your finances.

$\mathcal{D}ay$ 10

Worrying

Matthew 6:25–27 *"Therefore I tell you, do not be anxious about your life, what you will eat or what you will drink, nor about your body, what you will put on. Is not life more than food, and the body more than clothing? Look at the birds of the air: they neither sow nor reap nor gather into barns, and yet your heavenly Father feeds them. Are you not of more value than they? And which of you by being anxious can add a single hour to his span of life?..."*

~Prayer Starter~

"Lord, every day I find myself becoming anxious or worrying about things that are in my control and those that are out of my control. I worry about my bills, my family, myself and even find myself worrying if I will have the things that I need. God, help me to realize that you will supply all of my needs according to your riches and glory. Help me understand that I can trust you and that if you make sure the birds of this world are taken care of then you of course see me as well and will take care of me..."

~ Reflection ~

What do you find yourself worrying about the most? Why do you worry? Write down all of your anxious thoughts and give them over to God. Release all the worry to Him. I promise He will sustain you.

Psalm 55:22 *"Cast your cares on the LORD and he will sustain you; he will never let the righteous be shaken...."*

Day 11

Purpose

Jeremiah 29:11 *"For I know the plans I have for you,"
declares the LORD, "plans to prosper you and not to harm you,
plans to give you hope and a future..."*

~Prayer Starter~

"God, I want to live for you and know the specific purpose you have
for me in this life. I am here for your purpose and want to be in your
perfect will. Show me what you have called me to do in this life and give
me the patience to trust your plan. Every day I want to be in your purpose
and completely guided by you. Show me the gifts you have placed
specifically in me. Show me the talents you want me to use for your
glory..."

~ Reflection ~

Take a gift assessments test to get an idea of where you stand out in
your gifts. What would you do even if you weren't getting paid for it?
What are you most passionate about? You can find a gift assessments test
simply by searching *Spiritual Gifts Assessments Test* online. Multiple
choices will appear and you can pick the best fit for you. Ask God to
reveal the calling He has for your life. When you are walking in the
perfect will God designed for your life ; you will find true fulfillment.

Day 12

Others

Philippians 2:4 *"Do not merely look out for your own personal interests, but also for the interests of others..."*

John 15:12 *"This is My commandment, that you love one another, just as I have loved you..."*

~Prayer Starter~

"Lord, living in the selfish world we live in today, it is easy for me to look out for my own interests and forget that we are all here for each other and to show the love of Christ. God, help me to not just focus on myself, but focus on the needs of others around me. My family, friends, and even the needy. God, use me as a vessel to bless others and to provide a need for someone who is lacking. Help me to be more conscious of others and realize that when I help others I am also helping myself..."

~ Reflection ~

What things do you hold on to the most and find hard to share with others? When was the last time you worked for a charity or volunteered your time? What changes can you make to be more conscious of the needs of others around you? God has commanded us to love others as we love ourselves. He knows how important it is for us to be conscious of others' needs and bear each other's heartaches.

Day 13

Fellowship

<u>**Hebrews 10:25**</u> *"Not forsaking the assembling of ourselves together, as the manner of some is; but exhorting one another: and so much the more, as ye see the day approaching..."*

~Prayer Starter~

"God, thank you for the love of others and bringing those around me who care for me and encourage me. God, being single, sometimes I get used to being alone and forget the importance of having others around for accountability and support. Sometimes I forget how important it is to fellowship with likeminded people to help keep me on track and focus on my love towards Christ. Remind me always that I need others and most of all people need me as well. Remind me the importance of being involved with a church and coming together to worship you and abide in your presence and Word..."

~ Reflection ~

Why do you find yourself preferring to keep to yourself instead of fellowshipping with others? Is fear behind your reasoning of staying to yourself? What do you fear about getting close to others? Do you attend church regularly or some form of spiritual togetherness with like-minded individuals? Fellowshipping with others will give you accountability and support when you most need it.

Day 14

Need to Control

1 Peter 5:7 *"Cast all your anxiety on him because he cares for you..."*

Matthew 11:28 *"Come to me, all you who are weary and burdened, and I will give you rest..."*

~Prayer Starter~

"Lord, everyday things come up in my personal life and work life that I feel the need to fix, but I can't. It's hard for me to understand what exactly is going on and I can't do anything about it. I am used to controlling what goes on around me, and when I have control, I feel safe and trust the situation. God, help me to cast all of my concerns, problems, and plans over to you. Help me realize that I don't have to control everything around me because you are the author and finisher of my life and you have it figured out. Help me to also trust others with my life and give me discernment to know whom I can trust and who is being led by your spirit. I want to be able to have peace and know that regardless of what is happening around me, and though some things may seem out of control, you always have EVERYTHING under control and will take care of my every need..."

~ Reflection ~

What areas in your life do you not trust others to control or plan out? Why do you feel the need to control your environment? Do you only trust yourself? If so, why is that? Do you trust God to take care of you?

Find scriptures that reaffirm the care God has for you and also scriptures that reaffirm your trust in Him. Write them out and memorize them. Every time you feel things are out of control recite these scriptures to yourself and experience the peace in knowing your Father has it all under control.

_____

_____

_____

_____

_____

_____

_____

_____

_____

_____

_____

_____

_____

Day 15

Motherhood

Proverbs 31:28 *"Her children arise and call her blessed; her husband also, and he praises her..."*

~Prayer Starter~

"God, thank you for blessing me with the opportunity to one day be someone's mother and caregiver. Being a mother seems to be a lot of work and I sometimes question if I can truly be the type of mother like **Proverbs 31**. It seems like a lot of work and I am unsure if I am up for a task like that! God if your will for me to mother a child one day I pray you show me areas now that I can adjust to prepare me for motherhood. Show me the importance of selflessness. Show me the importance of loving your child more than you love yourself. I know you don't expect us to be perfect and will give me everything I need to care for a child. I know it is your will for us to multiply and create more servants for you, Lord. Help me to not fear motherhood and to approach it with joy and as a blessing. Prepare me and my husband now to be parents and reaffirm to us that you will make us strong where we are weak..."

~ Reflection ~

Do you wish to have kids one day? How are you now with kids? What qualities in your own mother do you want to carry over to your children and what qualities do you not? Write out what you feel is the perfect mother and compare them to **Proverbs 31**? Is it possible to be perfect?

No. But always have a goal to strive for and seek God to mold you and help you in this role if His will.

_____

_____

_____

_____

_____

_____

_____

_____

_____

_____

_____

_____

_____

_____

Day 16

Marriage

Mark 10:6–9 *"But from the beginning of the creation God made them male and female ^{7} For this cause shall a man leave his father and mother, and cleave to his wife; ^{8} And they twain shall be one flesh: so then they are no more twain, but one flesh. ^{9} What therefore God hath joined together, let not man put asunder..."*

~Prayer Starter~

"Marriage is something I truly desire, Lord, and if your will, I know you will grant the desires of my heart when the time is right. God, reveal to me the true meaning of marriage and your purpose intended. I see divorce around me all the time and I truly don't believe that is your will. Show me now the secret to keeping a marriage together and help me understand the importance of grace and mercy for the other. You gave Adam a helpmate for his good and I know that, if it's your will, you will bring me a helpmate for my good. I want a marriage dedicated to you and never ending. Reveal to me how to prepare for marriage..."

~ Reflection ~

Why do you want to be married? Do you feel your intentions are of the right spirit? What do you expect from your spouse in a marriage? As you read through *Single to Married*, the book, take notes of the areas in marriage you were unaware of and, needed areas of improvement.

Day 17

Discernment

1 Samuel 16:7 *"Do not consider his appearance or his height, for I have rejected him. The LORD does not look at the things people look at. People look at the outward appearance, but the LORD looks at the heart..."*

Hebrews 4:12 *"For the word of God is living and active, sharper than any two-edged sword, piercing to the division of soul and of spirit, of joints and of marrow, and discerning the thoughts and intentions of the heart..."*

~Prayer Starter~

"Lord, you see people for who they truly are and know their intentions without even hearing a word from them. You see their heart and I pray that you help me to be able to see the same. Whether someone I'm dating, or even just those who come around me as friends, help me to discern people and their spirits and not be naïve to their true intentions. Give me the wisdom to recognize good from evil and not ignore the red flags you show me. Help me to not let my desires crowd my mind so much that I miss people for who they truly are. Reveal to me who is in my life for a season and those who are in my life for a lifetime. I know you have a purpose for every action that comes towards me. Remind me of the importance of studying your word to attain wisdom..."

~ Reflection ~

Do you feel you have a good discernment for people and their intentions in your life? Think of a time in the past that you were wrong about an individual's intention in your life. What do you think caused you to be blind to their true intentions? Are you able to recognize the difference between good and evil?

For you to be able to discern others you have to know God's Word and know what a person of good nature looks like and the fruits they should bear. To do that, you have to fellowship with those who are of good nature to be able to recognize those who are not and most of all you have to fellowship with God.

_____

_____

_____

_____

_____

_____

_____

_____

_____

_____

Day 18

Fruits of the Spirit

Galatians 5:22–23 *But the fruit of the Spirit is love, joy, peace, forbearance, kindness, goodness, faithfulness, [23] gentleness and self-control. Against such things there is no law...*

~Prayer Starter~

"Seeing the fruits of the spirit, Lord, I see already that I have some areas in my life that need to improve. Some of the fruits I feel I am great at exuding while others I struggle with day to day. God, help me to learn how to develop my spirit in a way that is pleasing to your sight. Show me the areas where I am weak and reveal to me why I struggle with exuding some while excelling in others. I know you do not expect perfection, for that is why I have grace and mercy. Forgive me where I have not portrayed someone of the spirit of Christ and continue to work on me and refine me into your perfect work..."

~ Reflection ~

Looking at the fruits of the spirit, which do you find hard to carry out each day? What can you do to improve in this area and who can hold you accountable to this change? What can you do each day to keep in mind the importance of exuding the fruits of the spirit?

Write out this scripture and place it somewhere you can see each day. I had a coworker of mine who kept it in her sight every day, so that every time she interacted with someone, whether they were rude or not, she wanted to ensure she was in the right spirit.

Day 19

Forgiveness

__Ephesians 4:32__ *"And be ye kind one to another, tenderhearted, forgiving one another, even as God for Christ's sake hath forgiven you..."*

~Prayer Starter~

"Lord, many have hurt me in the past and there are those who have offended me and offend me daily. It is so hard sometimes to let go of some things others have done to me and I am having a hard time to forgive them. God, your Word says that we have to forgive others so you can forgive us as well. You show us grace when it is underserving. Help me to show grace to others when it is underserving as well. Regardless of what others have done to me we all deserve to be forgiven and look past each other's wrongs. Heal me from those who have hurt me and help me to forgive so I can move on and heal as well..."

~ Reflection ~

Who has offended you that you are still angry with? What offense was done that you are still hurting about and need healing? Go to God about this person and also the offense. God truly does care about the harm that was done to you, but it leaves no excuse to not forgive, regardless of what the offense may be. I know that's hard to accept, especially if we feel the offense was unjustified. But ask God to work on your heart and find a place to forgive them. You will be set free by forgiving them.

Day 20

Battle of the Mind

Philippians 4:8 *"Finally, brethren, whatever is true, whatever is honorable, whatever is right, whatever is pure, whatever is lovely, whatever is of good repute, if there is any excellence and if anything worthy of praise, dwell on these things..."*

Romans 12:2 *"And do not be conformed to this world, but be transformed by the renewing of your mind, so that you may prove what the will of God is, that which is good and acceptable and perfect..."*

~Prayer Starter~

"Lord, I want my thoughts to be of pure and righteous nature. God, throughout the day I have thoughts that I know are wrong, evil, and definitely not of good report. I want to keep my thoughts pure and acceptable to your sight. Lord, help me to transform my mind to think of your Word, your goodness, and anything that is of good report. Help me understand that I cannot control thoughts from coming to my mind but I can control focusing and festering on thoughts and evil plans. Be with me every second of the day and help me to recognize when my thoughts are not pleasing to you…"

~ Reflection ~

What do you find yourself focusing on throughout the day? Are they things that you wouldn't be ashamed to think of if God was right there with you? Guess what; He is. What thoughts do you struggle with that are not of God? Ask God to renew your mind and purify your thoughts. Memorize scripture that speaks the truth about the thought. For instance, if you think impure sexual thoughts, find scriptures on sexual purity. If your thoughts are of envy or lust, find scriptures that remind you of the importance of not idolizing things on earth. Do this with any thoughts you are struggling to control and speak the scripture each time it comes to mind. When I have thoughts that are not of good report I repeat this scripture to myself.

Psalm 19:14 *"Let the words of my mouth and the meditation of my heart be acceptable to your sight. Oh Lord my strength and my redeemer..."*

_____

_____

_____

_____

_____

_____

_____

_____

_____

_____

Day 21

Forgiving Myself

Isaiah 1:18 *"Come now, let us settle the matter," says the LORD. "Though your sins are like scarlet, they shall be as white as snow; though they are red as crimson, they shall be like wool..."*

~Prayer Starter~

"Lord, I have a past and I find it hard to forget it. Some people around me always remind me of who I was and sometimes I even find myself being reminded of who I use to be and the sins I committed. Lord, your Word says that you have forgiven me; that you have made my sins as white as snow. Not only do you forgive me but you also forget. Lord, help me to forgive myself just as you have forgiven me. Help me to use my past for a purpose instead of condemning myself for the mistakes I've made. Remind me always that condemnation comes from the enemy, but loving conviction comes from you. Help me to forgive myself and move on to the new life you have given me. You have made me a new creature and I need to forget the old..."

~ Reflection ~

What sins have you committed in the past that you still condemn yourself about? Are there people around you reminding you of your past actions or character? Why do you think it is so hard to forgive yourself, even though God has already forgiven you? If there are people around you reminding you of your old self, remove yourself from that negativity or either let them know your stance on the issue. God has already forgiven you, and not only that, He has forgotten. When God forgives you, and you repent, He does not see you as the old person anymore but covered in grace and a new creature. Forget the things of the past for your God is doing a new thing!

Day 22

Bitterness

Ephesians 4: 31-31 *"Let all bitterness and wrath and anger and clamor and slander be put away from you, along with all malice. Be kind to one another, tenderhearted, forgiving one another, as God in Christ forgave you..."*

~Prayer Starter~

"Lord, I've been by myself for a while now and haven't had a man in my life for a while. I've had bad experiences with guys of my past and, honestly, have gotten to the point where I don't trust them and I feel guarded. I didn't realize until now that I am angry about something and have become bitter and want to release myself from this hurt. God help me to let go of whatever pain I am holding on to from my past. Help me to forgive them and also learn to trust others again. I truly desire for companionship and a family but just have been in fear all these years. Show me how to remove bitterness from my heart and experience a life of freedom and love..."

~ Reflection ~

Why do you feel you are bitter? Did someone in particular cause this bitterness, or has it been an accumulation of people and wrongdoings towards you? Do you want to be free from this anger? A large part of bitterness has to do with anger, resentment, and un-forgiveness towards others. Ask God to heal you from the pain and help you to forgive the wrongdoing. Bitterness can steal so much joy from your life and it isn't hurting anyone in the process but yourself. Forgive them. Forgive the offense. Receive healing and receive your freedom.

_____

_____

_____

_____

_____

_____

_____

_____

_____

_____

_____

_____

_____

_____

Day 23

The Proverbs 31 Woman

Proverbs 31:10 *"Who can find a virtuous woman? For her price is far above rubies..."*

~Prayer Starter~

"Wow. This lady of Proverbs is pretty amazing and quite intimidating, God. I feel that I am so far from being someone like that and honestly don't see how I could do all of those things. God, show me what you are trying to reveal to the women you have created and what you want me to take from this scripture. I want to be a woman that children praise and a woman a husband is proud to have by his side. I want to be a woman of virtue. A one of a kind woman that is hard to find. Help me to take the qualities I have and mold them into the mother, wife, woman of Christ you have called me to be. Help me believe in myself and realize that I can be virtuous too and that it isn't about everything the woman did in this passage but it is about the heart in the woman. Mold my heart into a woman of virtue..."

~ Reflection ~

What intimidates you the most about **Proverbs 31**? Do you think you need to do every single thing this woman does to be virtuous? What qualities do you feel you have already that exude a virtuous woman? What areas can you improve? Realize that God does not expect you to do every single action this woman has performed. It is about having the heart

---

of a virtuous woman and the works will simply follow. He just wants to give you an idea of how a woman should present herself and represent her family. He wants you to see the love the woman has for her family and those around her and that a woman should be about building her character and spirit, not over concerning herself with physical beauty that fades.

_____

_____

_____

_____

_____

_____

_____

_____

_____

_____

_____

_____

_____

Day 24

Fear

2 Timothy 1:7 *"For God hath not given us the spirit of fear; but of power, and of love, and of a sound mind..."*

Isaiah 41:10 *"Fear thou not; for I am with thee: be not dismayed; for I am thy God: I will strengthen thee; yea, I will help thee; yea, I will uphold thee with the right hand of my righteousness..."*

~Prayer Starter~

"Lord, every day I find myself worrying and in fear of the unknown. I fear if I will ever get married. I fear if I will be a good wife and mother. I fear losing my job, taking care of my bills, losing my parents, my health, and the things I have no control over. God, help me to not let my fear drive me to do things that are unhealthy for me and help me to realize I can trust you. You are my provider and are aware of everything I need. Remind me that I should not fear losing anything or anyone on earth because as long as I have you, I am always covered. Lord, keep me from doing things that are not pleasing to your sight to gain attention from others because of my fear of being alone or accepted. You will fill any void that I have and you accept me for exactly who I am. Your Word says that you loved me first and knew me in the womb. There is no love like yours..."

~ Reflection ~

What things do you find yourself in fear about? What do you think drives your fear? Most of our fears are embedded in not trusting others with our lives, nor God. When we realize how much God loves you and sees every single detail in your life you will receive so much peace and reassurance. Every time you find yourself in fear of something repeat the verses above to yourself. You will quickly be reminded that the spirit of fear comes from the enemy, not God.

_____

_____

_____

_____

_____

_____

_____

_____

_____

_____

_____

_____

Day 25

Fighting Temptation

1 Corinthians 10:13 *"There hath no temptation taken you but such as is common to man: but God is faithful, who will not suffer you to be tempted above that ye are able; but will with the temptation also make a way to escape, that ye may be able to bear it..."*

~Prayer Starter~

"God, sometimes it is such a struggle to fight temptations in my life. Sometimes it feels impossible to live right and not fall into sin. Sex is everywhere around me. Greed is everywhere around me. Gossip, lust, envy, profanity; everywhere I look, temptation is right there ready to attack. God, I know that you wouldn't command us to do anything that isn't possible with your strength and you will always provide us a way to bear it and overcome it. Lord, help me to stop (Insert here your personal sin you are struggling with). I truly want to be molded like Christ and find it so hard to carry out your will and righteousness on earth. God, I know I can do this with you, for your Word says that I should glorify in my infirmities for where I am weak you make me strong. Show me how to fight this temptation. Strengthen my spirit so that it has control of my actions and not my flesh. I have victory in you in Jesus Name..."

~ Reflection ~

What temptations are you struggling with? What is the root of the temptation? Do you have friends, family members, or coworkers with whom you find yourself falling into the temptation? Who or what may you need to let go of so you can be free from this temptation? Find scriptures that deal specifically with the temptation you are struggling with. There are many books, scriptures, and insight on how to handle struggling with specific sins and temptations. If you are dealing with sexual sin I suggest my book *Not Tonight: My Worth Is Far Above Rubies.* I go over my personal struggle with sexual temptation and give you tips on how to overcome them. Know that you can overcome any sin or temptation you have been struggling with. Do not let the enemy tell you any different! You have victory in Jesus Name!

Day 26

Wisdom

James 1:5 *"But if any of you lacks wisdom, let him ask of God, who gives to all generously and without reproach, and it will be given to him..."*

~Prayer Starter~

"Father, your wisdom surpasses anything I could ever understand or fathom on this earth. I know you are alpha and omega; you are omnipresent and you are omniscient. You know everything that we need and you know the internal issues that we cannot understand. Lord, I pray you give me wisdom to help me in my walk on earth. Help me to see things the way you do. Help me to not lean on the wisdom of the world but the wisdom of the Word. Help me at work with every task that is given to me. Instead of trying to approach it with my own knowledge remind me to always go to you as well to open my eyes to things I don't see. Give me wisdom in dating. I want to be with a man that is good for me and won't stray me away from my relationship with you. Help me to use wisdom instead of being blinded by my desires to be with someone. Give me wisdom on how to handle issues in every aspect of my life: work, family, school..."

~ Reflection ~

When you are approached with an issue or problem, where do you go first to seek answers? Have you always been able to fix an issue without the help of others or Christ? Start making it a habit to seek God in every decision of your life. Before you take action on any situation, stop, pray, and ask God to give you understanding and to order your footsteps. That way you know for sure that you are being led by Christ.

Day 27

Past

Isaiah 43: 18-19 *"Do not call to mind the former things, Or ponder things of the past. Behold, I will do something new, Now it will spring forth; Will you not be aware of it?..."*

~Prayer Starter~

"God, thank you for loving me enough to give me a new beginning and a fresh start in my life, regardless of what my past has been. Lord, so many things have happened to me in the past that I am trying to let go of, but I am still struggling. I want to move on with my life and receive the great things you have in store, but I am scared of being hurt. My fears are holding me back from the opportunities you have placed before me and I don't have the strength to make that first move. Lord, continue to help me forgive those who have offended me and the things that were done. Help me to forgive (Insert Names of those who Hurt You). Help me to forgive them for (Insert Action/Harm that was done). Heal me in Jesus Name. Remove the hurt and offense from my mind and soul and help me receive my restoration, my healing, my new beginning. Lord, help me to not place my past on my future purpose, nor on the people you bring into my life for the good. Each day, walk with me and remind me of what you have ahead of me instead of what is behind me..."

~ Reflection ~

What past people have hurt you? What past actions have occurred that are holding you back from stepping out on faith and receiving what God has for you? Is it a new job you are scared of? A new mate that is entering your life? Maybe you are in fear of being a bad mother because of your own past experiences. Whatever the issue may be, give that fear over to Christ and leave your past exactly where it needs to be; the past. If you notice the scripture in **Isaiah 43** ask, "Will you not be aware of it?" I truly believe that is there because God knows we hold on to our past hurts sometimes so much that we can't even see what he is placing right before us. Let it go. Don't miss the new beginning He is placing right before you. Will you see it?

_____

_____

_____

_____

_____

_____

_____

_____

_____

_____

Day 28

Generational Curses

Exodus 20:5 *"Thou shalt not bow down thyself to them, nor serve them: for I, the LORD thy God [am] a jealous God, visiting the iniquity of the fathers upon the children unto the third and fourth [generation] of them that hate me..."*

Galatians 3:13 *"Christ hath redeemed us from the curse of the law, being made a curse for us..."*

~Prayer Starter~

"Lord, I have noticed for some time that my family has dealt with the same temptation and issues for years. I have fought some of these battles myself and I don't want these same iniquities and hardships to pass along to my kids or their generation. God, I pray that you bind and break the spirit of (Insert hardship, sin, or struggle that is a trend in your family) and cast it into the sea. I pray that you take away any spirit that is not of you off of my family and generations to come and that we experience freedom. Reveal to us what the enemy is trying to place on our family and show us how to fight against it. Your Word says that we wrestle not against flesh and blood but against spirits and principalities. But when Christ died for our sins, we were immediately covered by his blood and I pray it covers us all. Thank you, Lord, for giving us the strength to remove these habits and start a new generational trend for my family..."

~ Reflection ~

What sins, transgressions, have you noticed your family dealing with? Did this same issue happen with other family members of the past? Is the sin still reoccurring, or are those family members dealing with the issue and receiving healing and recovering? Whether it's dealing with debt, sexual promiscuity, anger, depression, addiction or whatever the issue may be; God can break the curse of your family and it can start with you. All families have their different iniquities and they can sometimes go back generations and generations ago. Speak over your family. Speak life into your family. You can be the one person that breaks and binds the spirit that the enemy is trying to place upon your family and set them free for years to come.

_____

_____

_____

_____

_____

_____

_____

_____

_____

_____

Day 29

Sacrifice

Romans 12:1 *"Therefore, I urge you, brothers and sisters, in view of God's mercy, to offer your bodies as a living sacrifice, holy and pleasing to God—this is your true and proper worship..."*

Romans 5:3–4 *"Not only so, but we also glory in our sufferings, because we know that suffering produces perseverance; ⁴ perseverance, character; and character, hope..."*

~Prayer Starter~

"Lord, help me to understand how to love and sacrifice the way you did for us with your son, Jesus Christ. There is no greater love than to sacrifice for another, and that is hard for me to grasp and understand. Being in a place where I have to put my desires, needs, and comforts to the side for someone else is hard to fathom. It feels that I basically have to be uncomfortable for a moment to help someone else be comfortable and happy. Lord, help me to understand the joy and reward of sacrificing for others. Whether it's my family, husband, or even my friends, show me the glory in sacrificing for them and help me to deny myself for others. As a follower of Christ I have to sacrifice to follow you as well and want to be able to deny everything around me to follow you and your ways. Be with me, Lord. Help me to sacrifice in my love towards other, to truly portray the unconditional love you have towards me..."

~ Reflection ~

When was the last time you sacrificed something you wanted for someone else? Was it hard? Do you have a hard time seeing the reward in denying yourself for others? Learn to sacrifice your needs and desires now for others before you are married or have a family. Sacrificing is a huge part of partnership and motherhood. It will be easier for you to sacrifice for them when you have practiced doing it when you are single. It takes time, patience, and adjustments on your part, but the reward is so fulfilling. You will begin to find yourself taking joy in sacrificing your happiness for the joy of someone else's.

_____

_____

_____

_____

_____

_____

_____

_____

_____

_____

_____

Day 30

Spiritual Growth

<u>Colossians 1:9–10</u> *"For this reason, since the day we heard about you, we have not stopped praying for you. We continually ask God to fill you with the knowledge of his will through all the wisdom and understanding that the Spirit gives so that you may live a life worthy of the Lord and please him in every way: bearing fruit in every good work, growing in the knowledge of God..."*

<u>1 Peter 2:2</u> *"Like newborn babies, crave pure spiritual milk, so that by it you may grow up in your salvation, [3] now that you have tasted that the Lord is good..."*

~Prayer Starter~

"During my prayer time and communion with you each day, Lord, I pray that I draw closer and closer to you. Lord open my eyes to your Word and give me revelation that only you can reveal. I am no longer a child spiritually and want to continue to grow mature spiritualty. Help me to be disciplined in studying your word. Help me to never deny the importance of fellowshipping with other believers. Help me understand your commandments and give me the strength to walk them out. I know you understand what is best for me and want to give my soul rest in your ways. Teach me your ways Father..."

~ Reflection ~

Where do you feel you need to mature spiritually? Do you read your Word to understand God and His ways? Get to know God more by reading your Word and communicating with Him. Whether through adding an app to your phone, or some form of daily devotion, spend time with Him and you will become more like Christ. Pray often. That is your way of talking to God. The great thing about it is He will talk back. The more time you spend with God and getting to know Him, the more you will grow spiritually and become wiser.

_____

_____

_____

_____

_____

_____

_____

_____

_____

_____

_____

About The Author
"Be Enlightened by His Word and Encouraged by His Promises"

Chloe M. Gooden is a mentor, speaker, and author of *Not Tonight: My Worth Is Far Above Rubies*. She has spoken at events on the life of celibacy, sexual temptation, dating, and relationships. She is the creator and manager of **Her Worth Is Far Above Rubies**, a community which is focused on encouraging women who are celibate, single, brokenhearted, and divorced. She is from Birmingham, Alabama and graduated from Mississippi State University for her Bachelors and University of Alabama at Birmingham for her Masters. She is to attend Central Baptist Theological Seminary to pursue her Master's Degree in Divinity in Nashville, Tennessee this Fall. Her passion is to encourage and enlighten others through God's Word. She hopes to continue helping others to develop an intimate relationship with Christ.

CONNECT WITH US

Chloe M. Gooden

Facebook: Chloe M. Gooden
Instagram: @chloemgooden
Twitter: @chloemgooden

Her Worth is Far Above Rubies

Facebook: Her Worth Is Far Above Rubies
Instagram: @knowyourworthrubies
Twitter: @AboveRubiesUR

THANKS FOR READING!

WE INVITE YOU TO SHARE YOUR THOUGHTS AND REACTIONS!

Other Books by Chloe M. Gooden

Single to Married
Becoming Who You Are In Christ and a Better
Complement as a Potential Wife

Become a better you and be ready to take on dating, relationships, and marriage. You cannot be a complement to someone until you are complete in Christ.

```
BOOK
PICTURE
```

Single to Married exposes major mistakes of the single woman in dating and relationships. Helps you make better choices in choosing a mate. Opens your eyes to everything that marriage, and being a wife, truly encompasses. Guides you in finding who you are and who God has called you to be. Shows you how to receive the life of fulfillment through healing, restoration, and a relationship with Christ.

Not Tonight
My Worth Is Far Above Rubies

Struggling in the Life of Celibacy?
Finding It Hard to Fight Sexual Temptation?

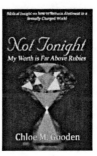

Not Tonight guides you through your journey of Celibacy, Sexual Addictions, and Temptation. This book will give you biblical insight, dating tips, and instruction to help you remain pure in your walk. This is a much needed eye opener to any Adult, Young Adult and Teen who is single, dating, or in a relationship.

CPSIA information can be obtained at www.ICGtesting.com
Printed in the USA
LVOW10s2122070714

393310LV00014B/180/P